SCOOBY-DOO'S™ GUIDE TO CAMPING

GHOST STORIES, GAMES & S'MORE!

sourcebooks
jabberwocky

 WELCOME

Did you know that when Scooby-Doo and his friends aren't busy solving mysteries, they love to go camping? It's true, and each friend in the Mystery, Inc. gang brings something special to every camping trip. Fred drives the Mystery Machine and knows lots of fun ways to pass the time while the gang is heading to the campsite. Daphne likes to make creative and interesting crafts. Of course, Shaggy always makes the yummiest snacks, and Scooby is always happy to make sure those snacks get eaten. And when nighttime comes and everyone gathers around the campfire, Velma tells the best stories. Sometimes they're a little spooky, but they always end with a big laugh.

Lucky for you, the Mystery, Inc. gang wants to make sure your camping adventures are fun and safe. So keep reading to learn about some really cool and groovy ways to have a great time in the great outdoors!

Let the Fun Begin!

Before you start making your camping plans, you should take the Camp Scooby oath. What's an oath? An oath is like a promise you make to yourself. Read the oath Scooby wrote for you below. (Actually, Velma wrote it for Scooby. Scooby's a dog and has trouble holding a pen with his paws.) Even better, get everyone who's going on your camping adventure to read it aloud together!

THE CAMP SCOOBY OATH

I promise to be the best camper I can be.

I will follow the rules of the campsite,
because the rules help keep me safe.

I will appreciate nature and leave the
campsite clean so that all the other
campers and critters can enjoy it too,
especially a big brown dog
named Scooby-Doo.

Most of all, I will have fun, even if it rains
and my shoes get soggy and my snacks
get mushy.

A camper doesn't complain!

SCOOBY HELPS YOU PREPARE!

There are lots of different places to go camping, and lots of fun ways to enjoy the outdoors. Some campers travel miles away from home to a sleepaway camp, and some set up camp in their very own backyard. Whether you're sleeping in a tent, a cabin, a camper, or out under the stars, the best way to make sure you have an awesome time is by being prepared. The most important part of being prepared means making sure you pack all the things you'll need. Scooby's gone ahead and made a list of camping supplies for you!

Packing for Camp with Scooby

TENT
Sleeping outside is fun, but you never know when it's going to rain. A tent will keep you nice and protected. When Scooby was little, he loved his pup tent.

SLEEPING BAG
The ground can be hard and the night can be cold. Stay warm and cozy in your very own sleeping bag. You can also pretend you're a burrito. Scooby and Shaggy love burritos!

Sleeping Pad or Air Mattress

A sleeping pad or air mattress will help put a little room between you and the ground.

Pillow

A pillow will help you sleep, and you might even get into a silly pillow fight with your fellow campers... unless pillow fights are against the rules. Hope they're not, though!

Flashlight or Lamp

When the sun goes down, it can get really dark outside. A flashlight or battery-operated lamp can light the way. Remember, campers like to stay safe. Be sure you check the batteries before you set off on your adventure.

Chairs and Table

It's always good to bring folding chairs and a small table. Eating on the ground is fun, but you might end up sharing your snacks with an army of ants. If folding chairs and a table are too much to pack or carry, you can always bring a big blanket to throw on the ground. Just be sure to shake it out afterward so the ants know who's boss.

Jacket or Sweatshirt

The temperature can change when you're camping, especially at night. Bring something warm to wear. If you look good in it, that's even better. Scooby loves his Coolsville University sweatshirt.

HAT

During the day, you'll need something to protect you from the sun, and at night, you'll need something to keep your head warm. Scooby's favorite hat is his detective hat. It makes him look really smart.

SUNSCREEN

It's great to enjoy the sun, but it's not so great to end the day with a sunburn. Be sure to bring plenty of sunscreen, and be double sure to actually use it. You don't want to end up looking like a stop sign.

INSECT SPRAY

Unlike Scooby, you probably don't have a problem with fleas—but there are still lots of other bugs out there that might make you itch. Keep them away with a really good bug spray. If you do get bitten, tell an adult, and try not to scratch! Bug bites can itch, but scratching them only makes them itchier.

FIRST-AID KIT

This should be put together by an adult. When you get a scrape, a boo-boo, or a bite, an adult should be able to make you feel better by using the first-aid kit. Fred always keeps a first-aid kit full of bandages, medicine, and emergency Scooby Snacks in the Mystery Machine.

WATER

Whether you have plastic bottles or an old-fashioned canteen, it's important to drink lots of clean water.

TRASH BAGS

Awesome campers always remember to never leave a mess, so be sure to pick up any trash or litter. You also never know when you might end up with wet or damp clothes. You'll want to keep those separate from your dry clothes. Garbage bags are perfect for doing just that.

TOILET PAPER AND HAND SANITIZER

When you've got to go, you've got to go! And don't forget to clean your hands with sanitizer.

PLASTIC PONCHO OR RAINCOAT

Taking a shower is great, but not when you're wearing all your clothes. Keep dry and warm. Bring a poncho or raincoat just to be prepared.

FOOD AND GAMES

Of course, no camping trip is complete without lots of yummy food and plenty of games and activities! Fred, Velma, Daphne, and Shaggy are going to share some of their favorite games, activities, and recipes later in this book. You can make the perfect list of food and fun with their help.

Let's Check Scooby's List!

Here's a list of some of the things Scooby is planning to bring. Scratch out the items that he should probably leave at home.

- Flashlight
- Mirror
- Baseball cap
- Video game
- Television
- Sleeping bag
- Jacket
- Bandages
- Bed sheets
- Pillow
- Tuxedo
- Air mattress
- Roller skates
- Scooby Snacks
- Water dish
- Insect spray
- Hairdryer
- Sunscreen
- Fake beard
- Folding chairs

The Scooby-Dos and Scooby-Don'ts of Camping

Scooby wants you to have a great time, but he also wants you to stay safe. When you are out in nature, there are some things you should do to have fun as a courteous camper, and there are some things you shouldn't do so that you and your fellow campers stay healthy and don't get hurt.

SCOOBY-DOS

➡ *Have fun! That's why we go camping, isn't it?*

➡ *Explore! Nature is wonderful when you take time to notice all the little things. Just be sure you don't explore by yourself.*

➡ *Keep yourself and your campsite clean. Wash your hands and pick up after yourself. If you see litter, throw it away. That's what courteous campers do.*

➡ *Take pictures! You'll want to share your awesome adventures.*

➡ *Wear shoes. There are lots of things on the ground that can scrape, scratch, and even bite. Keep your feet protected.*

- *Stay in sight of the other campers at all times. If you can't see them, they can't see you. Don't make them worry.*

- *Be prepared for anything. It could rain. You could get a scraped knee. You could see wild animals. It's all part of camping, and smart campers are prepared for anything nature might bring.*

Scooby-Don'ts

- *Don't keep food in your tent. There are a lot of critters that can smell your delicious snacks, and you don't want them visiting you in the middle of the night. Zoinks!*

- *Don't eat any berries or nuts from the trees or bushes unless an adult says they're okay. There are lots of things that might look good to eat, but they can make you sick.*

- *Don't touch or grab leaves from any vines or bushes. Poison ivy, poison oak, and poison sumac are some of the itchiest, ickiest plants out there. If you start to itch or see a rash, tell an adult immediately.*

➡ *Don't feed, chase, or try to pet any woodland animal. They may look cute and cuddly, and they may even approach you, especially if you have food. But they may not be as nice as they seem. Some can bite, some can scratch, and some can spray you with a very stinky spray. Take a photo instead.*

➡ *Don't wander off alone. Remember to use the buddy system. Agree that you'll always stay near your buddy and your buddy will always stay near you. After all, Scooby is never far from Shaggy. That's just what friends do.*

FRED'S GROOVY TRAVEL ACTIVITIES!

As the official driver of the Mystery Machine, Fred knows that long trips can be boring. What does Fred do when the gang starts to sigh, pout, and ask, "Are we there yet?" He helps them play a game! Fred knows the gang loves solving mysteries, and his games help them sharpen their sleuthing skills. So are you ready for some travel fun? Let's see what mystery games Fred has planned for your trip!

I SEEK, YOU SEEK

This is a fun and easy travel game. Scooby loves it because he enjoys hanging his head out the window of the Mystery Machine to watch the world whizz by. But you're a human, so remember to stay buckled up in your seat.

This is how the game is played. One person thinks of an object (make sure it's not too easy), and then everyone else in the car looks out the window to see if they can guess the object. Just shout your guesses out loud! The winner then gets to pick the next object everyone has to seek. Here are some examples:

➡ *A black-and-white spotted cow with her calf*

➡ *A billboard with a picture of a dog on it*

➡ *A vanity license plate*

➡ *A smiley face*

➡ *A purple car*

➡ *A dog with his head out the window of another car*

➡ *A flock of birds*

➡ *A truck pulling a boat*

SCOOBY-DOOBY-CLUE

This game requires nothing but your smarts and a little creativity. First, you need to think of two rhyming words like *Bed Head* or *Silly Chilly* or *Potato Tomato*. Don't tell anyone the two rhyming words you've thought of. Next, you have to figure out how many syllables are in each word. *Bed Head* has one syllable in each word, so if this were your choice, you would announce to everyone that you have a SCOO-DOO.

By telling everyone you have a SCOO-DOO, you've given them a clue that the answer they have to guess is a pair of rhyming one-syllable words. Then you provide a second clue.

For example, you might tell everyone that the SCOO-DOO clue is "It's where I sleep and where I think." Everyone then takes turns guessing.

A SCOOBY-DOOBY is a pair of rhyming two-syllable words, like *Silly Chilly*. The most difficult is the dreaded three-syllable SCOOBIDY-DOOBIDY. Velma's really good at these. If the SCOOBIDY-DOOBIDY clue is "One makes the ketchup and the other makes the fries," what do you think the answer might be? If you guessed *Tomato Potato,* then you are really smart and really good at SCOOBY-DOOBY-CLUE.

If no one guesses the right answer, you might have to give the group another clue. Be creative, but don't make it too easy. Half the fun is making everybody use their detective brain to figure out what the clues mean.

Here's a list of some SCOO-DOOs, SCOOBY-DOOBYs, and SCOOBIDY-DOOBIDYs and their clues. Try them on your friends and family. Once you get really good, you can start making up your own!

SCOO-DOOS AND THEIR CLUES (EASIER):

➡ *The yummiest way to pick up leaves: Cake Rake.*

➡ *You can sit in it, but it might eat you: Chair Bear.*

➡ *It's what a vampire might wear on his head: Bat Hat.*

➡ *It's smaller than where a rat would live: Mouse House.*

SCOOBY-DOOBYS AND THEIR CLUES (A LITTLE HARDER):

➡ *It grows in a superhero's garden: Power Flower.*

➡ *It's what happens when you drop your lollipop on the beach: Sandy Candy.*

➡ *It's a town where everything purrs: Kitty City.*

➡ *It's what Scooby's stomach turns into when he eats too much: Belly Jelly.*

Scoobidy-Doobidys and Their Clues (really hard):

➡ *I bought a ticket and won a big ceramic bowl: Pottery Lottery.*

➡ *It happened a long time ago, but no one can figure it out: History Mystery.*

➡ *During the holidays, we do one of these to our house, and the other we do in our house: Decorate Celebrate.*

➡ *I keep hundreds of baseball cards in a locked box: Collection Protection.*

MISSING MIDDLE

The gang really likes this game, and they're sure you and your friends and family will enjoy it too! It starts with one player calling out a category. This player could say "Animals," or "Fruits," or "School Subjects." That's the first clue. The second clue is the first and last letter of the word in that category.

If Fred said the category was "Insects" and the first and last letters were B and E, what would you guess? If you guessed "Bee," you'd win! But if you guessed "Beetle," you'd still win, because it perfectly matches the clue: *an insect that starts with a B and ends with an E.* Whoever wins the first round gets to start the next one. Younger players who don't know the alphabet very well might need some help.

Here are some categories with Missing Middles. Try guessing these, and then try coming up with some of your own!

ANIMALS:

➡️ *O and H*

➡️ *H and S*

➡️ *T and R*

➡️ *M and Y*

VEGETABLES:

➡️ C and Y

➡️ L and E

➡️ O and N

➡️ T and O

CLOTHES:

➡️ H and T

➡️ P and S

➡️ S and S

➡️ G and E

ANSWERS:
Animals: Ostrich, Hippopotamus, Tiger, Monkey
Vegetables: Celery, Lettuce, Onion, Tomato
Clothes: Hat, Pants, Socks (or Shoes), Glove

Fred hopes you'll try some of these games to sharpen your sleuthing skills and your sense of fun. Before you know it, you'll be at the campsite with a new mystery to solve: where did all that time go?

DAPHNE'S ARTS & CRAFTS!

Daphne always has the coolest activities up her sleeve, and whenever the Mystery, Inc. gang goes on a camping adventure, they make lots of really wonderful gifts to give away when they get back home.

Daphne is never without her supplies. She carries them in a big plastic container in the Mystery Machine so they don't fall out or get mixed up with other camping supplies. She keeps the container sealed with a lid so that everything stays neat and dry.

MAKE YOUR OWN ARTS AND CRAFTS BOX

Here's a list of some of some of the art supplies Daphne always has in her craft box. What would you keep in yours?

➡ Crayons
➡ Safety scissors
➡ Glue
➡ Paint brushes of various sizes
➡ Yarn
➡ Popsicle sticks
➡ Markers (washable and permanent). Be careful with the permanent ones, because, well, they're permanent!
➡ Googly eyes
➡ Colorful pipe cleaners
➡ Magnets
➡ Glitter
➡ Blank paper for drawing and coloring
➡ Colored construction paper for cutting and folding
➡ Small plastic cups for brushes and paint
➡ Paper towels or napkins for cleaning up
➡ Paint (craft, water-based, or acrylic*)

*Acrylic paint works best for rock painting. The brighter the color, the better. Acrylic paint can be messy, so try not to get any on your clothes. You could wear an apron or smock.

Daphne's Art Supplies

CAMPING ROCKS!

After the gang unpacks the Mystery Machine and sets up camp, Daphne gives everyone a big plastic bucket to go on a rock hunt. Then they explore the campsite, making sure not to go too far. They fill their buckets with any cool rocks they find while exploring. (Before setting out on their rock hunt, the gang always checks the campsite rules to make sure that moving rocks is allowed.) When their buckets are full, they all meet back at the campsite. Daphne washes all the rocks in a bucket of water. Then she sets them out to dry in the sun.

Once the rocks are clean and dry, the real fun begins. Daphne opens her arts and crafts box, and the gang gets to work decorating their rocks with paint, markers, glitter, glue, crayons, and even yarn.

How to Decorate Your Rocks

Paint: If Shaggy thinks a rock is shaped like a ladybug, or an owl, or anything else, he paints it to look like just like that. Shaggy is always hungry, so most of the time he paints his rocks so they will look just like his favorite foods. One time he painted a bunch of flat, round rocks to look like pancakes. Then he glued them all together in a big stack! He's even glued magnets onto some of his smaller rocks so that he can put them on the refrigerator when he gets home.

Glitter: Velma likes to cover her rocks in sticky glue and then roll them in glitter so they sparkle. She also likes to glue googly eyes and pipe cleaners or small sticks to make antennae for her funny rock creatures.

Crayons: Fred has a really cool way of decorating rocks by the campfire. Fred is an adult, so he knows how to do this safely. You'll need an adult like Fred to help you if you want to decorate your rock with fire-melted crayons. First, you'll need to choose a few crayons and set them aside while the adult warms your rock very close to the campfire. Using tongs or an oven mitt, the adult then picks up the hot rock and puts it on a towel or on the ground in front of you. DON'T TOUCH THE HOT ROCK! Using one crayon at a time, you can draw on the hot rock. The crayon will melt and swirl and drip, making all sorts of really neat designs. Keep adding colors until the rock is too cool to melt the crayons.

Yarn: Daphne likes to wrap her rocks with colorful yarn, stringing or gluing beads or even sticks or acorns as she goes. When she's done, the rocks have been transformed into a fantastic rainbow of colors.

HAVE A ROCK SHOW

When the gang has finished painting and decorating their rocks, they like to place them all on a table. Scooby pretends he's an art judge. He looks at one rock and says, "Oooh!" He looks at another rock and says, "Ahhhh!" He's always impressed by his friends' artistic talents.

MAKING YOUR ARTWORK LAST

To make sure the gang's painted rocks last a long time, Fred will spray them with a sealer so the paint doesn't fade. He does this far away from the campfire and away from the wind because the sealer has icky fumes. If you want your painted rocks to last, you'll need an adult to do this for you.

SPY BOTTLE

This is one of Scooby's favorite craft projects! You'll need:

- A smooth, clear plastic bottle with a cap
- Uncooked rice, dry light sand, or dry beans (white rice works best)
- Paper and pen
- 10-15 small objects you've found while camping

Scooby had Velma write down all the objects on a small piece of paper, and then he glued the list to the bottom of the clear plastic bottle. He put all the objects in the bottle and filled it almost to the top with uncooked rice or dry light sand. He also could have used dry beans, but Shaggy was going to use those to make camp chili. Scooby then sealed up the bottle with the cap and gave it a shake to mix up all the objects. He now has a keepsake of his camping trip!

To make a Spy Bottle, Scooby first looks for 10–15 small objects at the campsite. The last time he went camping, he found:

- A black pebble
- A tarnished penny
- An acorn
- A tiny stick
- An old nail
- A piece of bark
- A feather
- A plastic bead
- A dragonfly wing
- A lost button

HOW TO PLAY WITH A SPY BOTTLE

First, give the Spy Bottle to a friend, who will then turn it up-side-down to read the list of objects inside. Then they have to keep turning the bottle and searching for the objects buried in the rice, sand, or beans until all have been found. Scooby has made Spy Bottles during all of his camping adventures, and he is very proud of his collection.

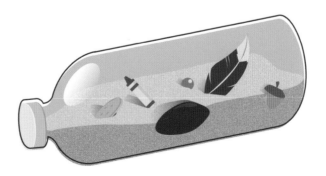

CRITTER COTTAGES

While a lot of art projects are made to take home and share with friends and family, Critter Cottages are left for woodland critters and other campers to find. What are they? These are tiny little houses or shelters you make for squirrels, mice, or even invisible woodland fairies. When the Mystery, Inc. gang sets out to make Critter Cottages, Daphne seals up the arts and crafts box because she knows the gang won't need it. Instead, each person gets a bucket to fill with whatever they can find to make the perfect Critter Cottage. Then they choose where each Critter Cottage will be built. Shaggy and Daphne stick twigs into the ground to make the walls of a hut, and then they use crisp leaves to make the roof. Fred and Velma stack rocks to make a sturdy cottage with a stick roof. Scooby makes a path between the two cottages with his big brown paws.

The gang is always careful when picking out their building materials. They never pull leaves off trees or bushes. They also try not to use anything that might be considered litter, especially anything made of metal or plastic, or any food items that might attract animals too big to live in the Critter Cottage.

The gang loves discovering Critter Cottages left behind by other campers...or maybe, just maybe, they were left behind by invisible forest fairies? *Jinkies!*

SCOOBY LOVES CAMPING GAMES!

Scooby loves the great outdoors. As soon as the Mystery, Inc. gang arrives at the campsite, Scooby is ready to explore and play games. Unlike Scooby, you can enjoy these activities on two feet, not four.

A-TO-Z PHOTO SAFARI

Velma is never without her camera, and when the gang goes camping, she and Scooby love going on an A-to-Z Photo Safari! To go on your own A-to-Z Photo Safari, you must take at least 26 photos, one for each letter of the alphabet. You should also bring a pencil or pen and a small notepad with the entire alphabet in a list. If you take a photo of a tree, you'd write "tree" next to the letter T. If you take a photo of a pond, you'd write "pond" next to the letter P. Your Photo Safari doesn't end until every letter in the alphabet has something written next to it. Some letters are harder than others to fill. It's hard to find a xylophone while camping. Velma puts Scooby in charge of finding what they need for their photos. When they take a photo of something they don't know the name of, they usually make up a name for it, using some of the harder-to-find letters like X, V, Q, or Z.

After the camping trip is over, Velma prints up the photos and puts them in an album to share with friends. Here are some of her favorites!

Z is for Zooby-Doo

C is for Canoe

O is for Opossum

FIND AND FOUND

No one in the gang is better at finding things than Scooby-Doo, and no one loves looking for things more than everyone's favorite big brown dog. Fred makes it extra fun by hiding some of Scooby's favorite toys around the campsite, keeping a list of the things Scooby has to find. Then he does the same thing for Shaggy, Velma, and Daphne, keeping a different list for each of them. And then the real fun begins. Starting at the top of each list, Fred tells each person what they should be looking for.

Velma looks for her eyeglass case, while Scooby looks for his squeaky toy. Daphne looks for her favorite hair bow, and Shaggy looks for his yo-yo. When the players find hidden objects, they bring them to Fred, who marks them off the list. Then Fred tells them what object they should be looking for next. The first person who finds everything on their list wins! The winner then joins someone else to help them with their list. When everything is found, the game is over. Here's a list of some of the things the gang had to find:

SCOOBY:

▶▶ *Squeaky toy*

▶▶ *Water dish*

▶▶ *Teddy bear*

▶▶ *Tin whistle*

VELMA:

- *Eyeglass case*

- *Magnifying glass*

- *Bug spray*

- *Book about plants*

DAPHNE:

- *Hair bow*

- *Lipstick*

- *Fashion magazine*

- *Campsite map*

SHAGGY:

- *Yo-yo*

- *Cookbook*

- *Plastic spoon*

- *Flashlight*

To play your own game of Find and Found, ask your campmates to give you four or five things they've brought with them on the trip. Then hide these things all around the campsite. Keep a separate list for each person who is playing. You might need to write down where you hid everything (or make a map), just in case your friends can't find what they're looking for. If someone has a hard time finding his or her object, you can give clues or let the player know whether the object is nearby by saying "hot" (if it's close) or "cold" (if it's not).

FLICKER-FLICKER-FLASH!

When the sun goes down, the fun doesn't need to stop! Daphne gives everyone a flashlight for a game of Flicker-Flicker-Flash! To start, everyone agrees to the boundaries of the game. They try to choose an area within the campsite that isn't too far away. After all, this is a nighttime game, and they don't want anyone to fall or get hurt by going out too far.

Scooby loves being "It," so the first round usually starts with Scooby covering his eyes and counting to ten while the gang hides around the campsite. When Scooby uncovers his eyes, he shouts, "Flicker!" Everyone who is hiding turns on their flashlight, waves it around for a few seconds, and then turns it off again. Scooby moves through the dark toward where he thinks he saw people hiding. He can't turn on his flashlight. Once he thinks he's close to the group he shouts, "Flicker!" Once again, the group has to quickly turn their flashlights on and off. Scooby moves toward the lights again. Once he thinks he's found someone, he points his flashlight in their direction, turns it on, and shouts, "Flash!" If Scooby's light hits one of the players, then that person becomes "It" and they have to begin counting to ten while everyone else hides. If Scooby's light doesn't hit anyone, then everyone scurries to a new hiding spot while Scooby covers his eyes and counts to ten again.

SHAGGY'S CAMP SNACKS!

If there's one thing Shaggy loves almost as much as his friend Scooby, it's snacks! And no camping trip is complete without delicious and fun-to-make treats. Lucky for you, Shaggy always has some really yummy recipes that are perfect to share and enjoy with other happy campers.

Remember the rules of camping. Keep your food out of your tent, maybe locked in an icebox. You don't want critters smelling your delicious creations and spoiling the fun by stealing everyone's treats.

Here are some of Shaggy's favorite recipes!

SQUISHY FUDGE

This sweet treat with a gross name is perfect for squeezing onto apple slices or crackers. You just can't go wrong with Squishy Fudge!

Here is a list of ingredients that you'll need:

- 2 tablespoons salted or unsalted butter
- 1 tablespoon confectioners' sugar
- 2 teaspoons cocoa powder
- A dash of vanilla extract
- A dash of salt (if using unsalted butter)

Put all the ingredients in a sealable plastic bag and close it. Then, like the name says, you *squish!* Velma likes to squish with her hands, Scooby uses his paws, and Shaggy puts it under his arm. *Gross!*

When the ingredients are all mixed together, you can cut the corner off the bag and then squeeze the fudge onto your favorite fruit or cracker for a sweet snack.

CAMPFIRE PIZZA-RINIS

Do you know what is Shaggy and Scooby's favorite food in the whole entire world? You guessed it! *Pizza!* But when they go camping, there aren't any pizzerias in the woods. So what do they do to satisfy their pizza cravings? They make delicious Campfire Pizza-rinis!

To make your Campfire Pizza-rinis, simply take your cracker, pita, or flatbread slice and smear a little bit of pizza sauce on it. Sprinkle a little cheese on top and add your favorite toppings. Scooby likes pepperoni and olives. Shaggy likes ham and pineapple. Then all you have to do is place your Pizza-rini in a pan or griddle (preferably cast iron) and have an adult place it near the fire to warm up. Once the cheese melts and begins to bubble, they're ready to set aside and cool a bit. Then it's chow time! *Yay!* Who needs a pizzeria when you can make your own, Shaggy style?!

With any recipe that requires fire, make sure you have an adult helping you. To make your own Campfire Pizza-rinis, you'll need:

- Flat crackers, pita bread, or any kind of flat bread that's been cut into slices
- 1 (24-ounce) jar pizza sauce
- 1 (16-ounce) bag shredded cheese (Mozzarella is yummy and gooey)

Any of your favorite toppings, such as:

- Pepperoni
- Peppers
- Olives
- Pineapple
- Ham
- Anchovies (Yuck!)
- Kale
- Broccoli
- Mushrooms

SCOOBY'S S'MOREGASBORD

Scooby and Shaggy love to eat s'mores, and when they go camping, they really, really love a good S'moregasbord! Let's get started!

First, you'll need several long sticks or skewers to roast your marshmallows from a safe distance. Then you'll want to put together a tray of all the fixings. Some of the ingredients you might want to include are:

For Your Crispy Outside:

Graham crackers

Cookies

For Your Gooey Inside:

1 (16-ounce) bag jumbo marshmallows for roasting

Milk chocolate, dark chocolate, or white chocolate

Candy bars

Chocolate chips

Sliced bananas

Cinnamon

Berries: blueberries, blackberries, strawberries, or even huckleberries (Whatever those are!)

Nut butter: peanut, cashew, almond, or hazelnut (unless someone in the group has allergies)

Your favorite jams or jellies

Gummy candies: bears, worms, fish, or even giraffes (Do they make gummy giraffes?)

Chocolate peanut butter cups

Bacon bits

Mixed nuts

Cream cheese

Cayenne pepper (Careful—this stuff is spicy!)

Can you think of another good s'more filling? Add it here.

Once you have your S'moregasbord tray put together, the real fun begins.

Slide a marshmallow or two onto your stick or skewer and hold it near the campfire, but not directly in the flame. Be patient while your marshmallow puffs up and gets nice and toasty. If it catches on fire, you'll just have to blow it out and start over.

Once your marshmallow is toasted to gooey perfection, you slide it onto the crispy outside of your choice. Careful! Your marshmallow will be *very hot*! Choose your crispy outside wisely. Velma likes graham crackers, while Daphne loves the taste of oatmeal cookies. Shaggy likes chocolate chip cookies, and Scooby likes plain sugar cookies.

With your toasted marshmallow on its crispy base, add your favorite toppings from the Gooey Inside list. Then top it all off with another graham cracker or favorite cookie.

Some of the gang's favorite s'more recipes are:

➼ **Fred's Hipper-Than-Hip S'mores:** *Fred adds bacon bits and dark chocolate to his toasted marshmallow sandwiched between crisp graham crackers. Tasty!*

➼ **Daphne's S'mores Mexicanos:** *Daphne sprinkles a little cinnamon and a tiny bit of cayenne over milk chocolate and marshmallow, sandwiching it all between two chocolate cookies. ¡Muy bueno!*

➼ **Scooby's Go Nuts S'mores:** *Scooby is a dog, so he shouldn't eat chocolate, but he still enjoys a good s'more. He loads two sugar cookies with peanut butter, bananas, and mixed nuts. Yum yum!*

➼ **Velma's European Delight S'mores:** *Velma smears cream cheese on one graham cracker, and sprinkles chocolate chips all over the top. Then she spreads jam on another graham cracker and covers it with sliced berries. She then sandwiches her toasted marshmallow between the two. Jinkies! That's delicious!*

➼ **Shaggy's Kitchen Sink S'mores:** *Shaggy has a tough time deciding what to put on his s'mores, so he puts as much as he thinks the cracker or cookie can hold. He likes trying different combinations. Zoinks! He's going to have a tummy-ache!*

STORYTIME WITH VELMA!

After a long and fun-filled day, the Mystery, Inc. gang gathers around to hear a good campfire story from Velma. Before she begins, she places a flashlight under her chin, which makes her face look a little eerie. Sometimes her stories are a just a little bit spooky, but they always have a funny ending. Sometimes she even gets the gang to help her tell the story. Velma hopes you'll be nice enough to share some of her favorite campfire stories with your own camping buddies!

THE HAUNTED PIZZA!

Scooby and the Mystery, Inc. gang had just returned to their home in Coolsville after solving the Case of the Haunted Bumper Cars. Everyone was tired and hungry, and as the sun began to set, Fred and Daphne began making dinner for the gang. What was on the menu? *Pizza!* But there was something *different* about this pizza. Something a bit *strange.* As Daphne began to roll out the dough, she heard a faint growling sound. When she stopped rolling the dough, the growling stopped too, but when she began rolling again, the growling sound returned. "It's probably just the wind," she said to herself. A terrible storm had started brewing outside.

By the time she'd finished rolling out the dough, the growling had faded away. Fred put the sauce, cheese, and toppings on the pizza, and he placed the pizza in the oven. Just then there was a sudden rumble, like the growl of an angry and dangerous animal. Velma came rushing from the other room. The sound had woken her from her nap.

"What was that?!" she said.

"You heard it too?" asked Daphne.

The rain outside began to fall. "It's probably just the storm," said Fred. He was trying to comfort Velma and Daphne.

"What's for dinner?" asked Velma. She opened the oven door and peeked inside.

GROWLLLLLL!

The sound was much louder now. It filled the room! Fred, Velma, and Daphne began to shake with fear.

"Close the oven door!" shouted Daphne. Velma slammed it shut and the growl stopped.

"There's something wrong with this pizza," said Fred, eyeing the oven with suspicion.

"Slowly open the door again," Daphne said to Velma. Velma's hands shook as she pulled on the handle. She cracked the door of the oven just enough for the room to fill with the delicious smell of crisp pepperoni and bubbly cheese.

GRRRROOOOOOOOWWWWLLLLL!

Fred, Daphne, and Velma nearly jumped out of their skin! Was this pizza haunted? Was it angry that it was about to be eaten? Or was it planning on eating them?

GRRRROOOOOOOOWWWWLLLLL!

Shaggy and Scooby came in from the other room.

"Hey, gang. When's dinner going to be ready?" asked Shaggy.

GRRRROOOOOWWWWWWLLLLL!

The sound made Scooby jump into the air and shudder.

Daphne and Fred held each other in fear.

Velma, however, calmly opened the oven door, filling the room with the delicious smell of fresh-baked pizza.

GRRRRRROOOOOOOOOWWWWWWWWLLLLLLLLL!

Just then, the gang all looked at Shaggy. They knew where the sound was coming from! They had heard a lot of scary noises on their adventures, but there was one noise that was scarier than all of them put together...

The sound of Shaggy's empty stomach!

THE CASE OF THE GHOST THIEF!

Will Jenkins, a really mean kid at school, once dared Velma to check out the old abandoned house at the end of the street. He said it was haunted by the ghost of its former owner, who hated kids and vowed to spend eternity trapping as many in the house as he could. Velma didn't believe him. He said he would buy her lunch for the rest of the year if she were able to get a photo of the ghostly specter. Velma wasn't scared, as she'd never believed that ghosts are real.

So, one day after school, Velma went to the old abandoned house. She thought Will Jenkins would meet her there, but he never showed up. It was starting to get dark and the front door was boarded shut, but a side window was wide open. Velma climbed through the window into the dark and creaky house, gripping her camera. She noticed that the back door had the biggest spider web she had ever seen.

As Velma was creeping up the stairs, she heard a creak and then a moan. She began to get scared. Just as she reached the top of the stairs, she saw a shadowy figure swoop down into the room. She panicked and dropped her camera, and then ran screaming out of the house.

The next day at school, Velma told Will Jenkins what happened. He told her that she was a "fraidy-cat" and that he had been late getting to the house. He said that he had found her camera, but when he went to pick it up, the ghost had grabbed it and then had flown through the back door of the house.

Will Jenkins said he wasn't afraid of the ghost and chased after it through the back door to get the camera, but the ghost was just too fast. Velma begged Will Jenkins to go back to the house with her to look for the camera, and he agreed.

That afternoon Velma and Will Jenkins climbed through the side window of the house. Velma noticed a lot of footprints on the dusty floor. The big spider web across the back door glistened in the bit of light that streaked in from the setting sun. Velma told Will Jenkins that she had seen enough, and asked him to give back her camera.

How did Velma know that Will Jenkins had taken the camera?

ANSWER: Will Jenkins was already in the house when Velma arrived. He was lying about chasing the ghost through the back door because the spider web was still there. Wouldn't he have broken through it getting out the back door?

BUILDING YOUR OWN CAMPFIRE STORY!

The Mystery, Inc. gang loves when Velma starts a story and then has everyone else finish it. How does it work? Well, Velma usually starts with a really good sentence like, "Once, I was waiting for the bus when I felt something in my pocket. I reached in to grab it and couldn't believe my eyes when it turned out to be…"

Then Velma passes the story to Shaggy, who has to make up the next part of the story. He might say, "…a wrapped bit of candy. I gave it a sniff to make sure it smelled okay. It actually smelled delicious, so I unwrapped it and popped it in my mouth, but then something unexpected happened…"

Shaggy then passes the story to Fred. Fred continues to make up the story: "It tasted awful, so I spat it out immediately. But then I looked at my hands and I couldn't believe what I saw…"

Fred then hands the story over to Daphne, who continues, "My hands began to look like paws and hair began to grow all over my arms, and my nose turned black and my ears grew longer, and when I looked in the mirror I found out I had turned into…"

Then Daphne hands the story to Scooby, who shouts, "Scooby-Dooby-Doo!" The whole gang laughs and then makes up another story.

This is a great way for everyone to have a chance to tell a story, and it's a lot of fun!

Here are some great sentences to start your very own story with your campmates.

- *Once upon a time, there was a very old man who lived in a castle with a great big...*
- *While walking into the store the other day, I noticed a big sign that read, "Free! Take one!" I couldn't believe that they were giving away...*
- *My friend has a dog that can do extraordinary things. One time we were at the park when his dog...*
- *I had a dream where I was able to fly. I flew high above my house with my arms stretched out like a bird. I loved it, but then all of a sudden something came at me from the clouds. It was a...*

REMEMBERING YOUR CAMPING ADVENTURES!

When the tent has been packed, all the snacks have been eaten, the campsite has been cleaned up, and Scooby and the gang pile back into the Mystery Machine to head home, the only thing that's left are happy memories. To make sure they remember their camping adventures, the gang likes to find ways to make keepsakes.

Here are some of the keepsakes the Mystery, Inc. gang has made. They hope you make some of your own to share with your family and friends!

FLOWER POWER

Daphne loves to remember all the beautiful flowers she finds in the woods. First she remembers to check the campsite rules to make sure that picking flowers is allowed, then she gathers some of her favorites. Daphne keeps a big book that she uses to press and dry her flowers so they will last and not wilt away. To press your own flowers, you'll need a book just like Daphne's. Place each flower between two pages of the book and then carefully close the book, placing something heavy on top to make sure the flowers are really squished. Leave the book alone for a couple of weeks, and when you open it, you'll have beautiful pressed and dried flowers. You can put your pressed flowers in a scrapbook, or you can glue them into an arrangement on a sheet of paper. Daphne's room is decorated with lots of pressed flowers, and each one makes her smile.

EASY-TO-MAKE SCRAPBOOK

Scooby and Shaggy use three-ring binders to make fun and easy scrapbooks of their camping adventures. They have a whole stack of them at home, and on rainy days, they like to share them with the entire gang.

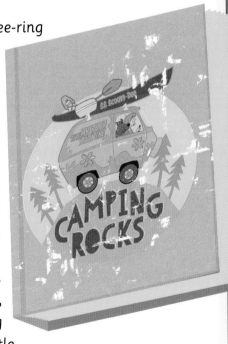

To put together your own scrapbook, you'll need photos from your camping adventure, along with a three-ring binder, safety scissors, glue, colored paper, markers, crayons, glitter, yarn, and some small camping mementos. (Mementos are little objects you can collect while you're on your camping trip: seashells, acorns, rocks, leaves, or anything else interesting you might have found.)

Once you've gathered up all your materials, you can start putting together your scrapbook. Think of it as telling a story—the story of your camping experience! Cut out photos and glue them to the colored paper. Use markers to write what you were doing and use crayons to draw little frames around each photo.

Glue some of your mementos to the sheets of paper. Be creative and have fun. It's *your* story!

Once you've used up all of your photos and mementos, punch holes in the colored paper and put the pages in your three-ring binder. Be sure to write your name, the name of the campsite, and the date of your trip on the cover of the binder. When you're all grown up, you can share your scrapbook with your kids and even your grandkids. You can also help them make scrapbooks of their own.

WRITE A STORY

Velma keeps a big book full of empty pages that she fills with stories about the Mystery, Inc. gang's adventures. She even includes some of her favorite photos. Velma loves to write, and if you do too, you can keep an adventure journal of your own. Good stories usually start at the beginning, work their way through the middle, and then end with something you've learned.

You can tell a good story by asking yourself questions. Maybe your story begins with finding out you're going on a camping trip. Ask yourself: *How did I feel about going camping? Who went with me? How did I get there?*

To write the middle of your story, you could ask yourself questions like: *What did I do while I was camping? Was there something that made me laugh? Was there something that made me scared? What was the best thing I ate? What was the worst?*

To finish your story, you could ask yourself: *Did I learn anything new? What will I remember most? What do I hope my next camping adventure will be?*